NONFICTION: WRITING FOR FACT AND ARGUMENT

NONFICTION: WRITING FOR FACT AND ARGUMENT

Journalistic Articles

Valerie Bodden

CREATIVE EDUCATION

Published by Creative Education

P.O. Box 227, Mankato, Minnesota 56002

Creative Education is an imprint of The Creative Company

www.thecreativecompany.us

Design and art direction by Rita Marshall

Production by The Design Lab

Printed by Corporate Graphics in the United States of America

Photographs by Corbis (Bettmann, Patrick Chauvel/Sygma, JP Laffont/Sygma, Swim Ink 2, LLC), Dreamstime (Ginasanders, Raja Rc, John Takai, Bogdan Wankowicz), Getty Images (Fox Photos), iStockphoto (Don Bayley, Trevor Hunt, Jose Luis Gutierrez, Pali Rao, Bruno Sinnah, Maria Toutoudaki)

Excerpt on page 32 from "In a Besieged Cambodian City, Hunger, Death and the Whimpering of Children" by Sydney H. Schanberg. From *The New York Times*, January 16, 1975, copyright © 1975 The New York Times. All rights reserved.

Excerpt on page 38 from "How to Lie with Statistics" by Darrell Huff from *Harper's Magazine*, August 1950. Copyright © 1950 by *Harper's Magazine*. All rights reserved. Reproduced from the August issue by special permission.

Library of Congress Cataloging-in-Publication Data

Bodden, Valerie.

Journalistic articles / by Valerie Bodden.

p. cm. — (Nonfiction: writing for fact and argument)

Includes bibliographical references and index.

Summary: An introduction to the ways that writers compose newspaper and magazine stories. Excerpts and analysis help to explain the importance of structuring and accuracy in this nonfiction form.

ISBN 978-1-58341-934-2

1. Feature writing—Juvenile literature. 2. Journalism—Authorship—Juvenile literature. I. Title. II. Series.

PN4784.F37B63 2010   808'.06607—dc22   2009024092

CPSIA: 120109 PO1094

First Edition

9 8 7 6 5 4 3 2 1

CONTENTS

The real world. We all live in it. But we don't all experience the same things. You probably have never flown in a space shuttle. You may never have been to China. And you certainly didn't live through the American Civil War. But you can read about these experiences and places in works of `nonfiction`—true stories about real life. Nonfiction has the power to show us what is happening—or what has happened—in our own city, in another country, or even in another era. It takes events or people from some corner of the world and helps us understand them—and see why we should care about them. Even as it informs us, nonfiction writing can make us feel deeply, laugh heartily, and see more clearly. And understanding the real world can help us to better understand our own lives.

Of all nonfiction publications, newspapers and magazines are probably the most abundant. Readers around the world rely on them as sources of both news and entertainment. Their pages are filled with articles presenting the stuff of real life, from wars and disasters to sports scores and celebrity sightings.

Yet just because newspaper and magazine articles are about real life does not mean they are easy to write. Journalists must carefully research or observe their topics and craft facts into an engaging text that compels readers to read on—often with a limited number of words and under a tight deadline. But when they do, the result is a more informed citizenry—and a more informed you!

People have always wanted to know what was going on in the world around them. The first news accounts were spread orally, but in the first century B.C., Roman citizens began to obtain their news from the *Acta Diurna* (*Daily Acts*) news bulletin, which was hung in the large public center known as the Forum. By the eighth century A.D., the Chinese were distributing news bulletins rather than hanging them in public places. These early news accounts—which conveyed official notices or court records—were handwritten, but in the 15th century, the development of the printing press made it possible to create large quantities of typewritten newsletters.

During the 1620s, the first English-language news-sheets were created in Holland and England, but it wasn't until 1665 that the *Oxford Gazette* became the first newspaper in the form we think of today. Newsletters also became common in Germany, Italy, and other European countries during the 16th and 17th centuries. In 1704, The *Boston News-Letter* became the first continuously published newspaper in America, and *The Boston Gazette* was formed shortly afterward. Both of these early papers focused largely on news from England, information that was at least two months old by the time

A 1702 issue of the British newspaper *The Daily Courant*

The Daily Courant.

Thursday, March 12. 1702.

From the Vienna Journal, Dated March 1. 1702.

Vienna, March 1.

THE Regiment of Huffars commanded by Major General Colonitz, confifting of 1000 Men, is on its March from Hungary towards Bohemia and the Empire; and several other Imperial Regiments are marching this way. Our new Levies are carry'd on with great Succefs, and Recruits are continually fending away to their refpective Regiments. We have Advice from Adrianople that the Sultan is in that City, and that my Lord Pagett, Embaffadour from England, is alfo arriv'd there from Conftantinople, and preparing to fet out for this Place in a few days. Count Teckely lives in fo Poor a Condition at Ifmid, otherwife call'd Nicomedia in Afia, the place to which he is banifh'd, that his Wife is reduc'd to Sell her Jewels for their Subfiftance; the Port having taken from them all their Eftate.

Copenhagen, Feb. 11. The French Embaffador is preparing for his Departure from hence, and feems very much diffatisfy'd with the Succefs of all his Negotiations at this Court: but chiefly, becaufe Seven new Regiments are raifing for the Service of the States General. There is a Report that the King intends in a fhort time to take a Journey to Holftein, and from thence to Norway.

From the Vienna Journal, Dated March 4. 1702.

Vienna, March 4. Our Forces defign'd for Italy continue their March thither with all Expedition, and our Army there will be much more Numerous this Year than it was the laft. The Levy-Money is diftributed to the Officers of the new Regiments of Huffars that are now raifing; and fome of them are to Serve in Italy, the others on the Rhine. Proveditore General Vorftern has laid up great Magazines of Provifions in the Countrey of Friuli; and having agreed with feveral Undertakers for the tranfporting of it from thence by the way of the Gulf of Venice towards the River Po; he has already fent into Italy by that means, about 60000 Bufhels of Oats, and 20000 of Wheat; fo that we do not in the leaft apprehend that our Army there can be in any Want of Provifions the next Campaign.

Warfaw, Feb. 19. We are fully convinc'd by two Letters which the King of Sweden has written to the Cardinal Primate, That that Prince is not in the leaft inclin'd to come to an Accommodation with us; which makes us fear that the Unfortunate breaking up of the Diet will foon be follow'd by a General Sedition. The hopes we were in that the Mufcovites would have given the Swedes fome Diverfion on the other Side of Narva, are vanifh'd; nor will Oginski's Party be able to hinder them from taking Poffeffion of Birfa. And tho' the Affairs of Lithuania are Adjufted, it caufes but little Joy among us, fince we evidently fee that neither Party have yet laid afide their Animofities.

From the Harlem Courant, Dated March 18.

Bruxelles, March 15. The King has made the following Promotion of General Officers, who are to Serve in his Army in Flanders the next Campaign. Don Andrea Benites, heretofore Colonel of the Guards of his Electoral Highnefs of Bavaria, and the Count D'Autel, Governor of Luxemburg, are made Lieutenant Generals: The Counts of Grebendonk and Toulongeon, the Barons of Winterfelt and Noiremont, Don John de Ydiaques, and Don Antonio Amenzaga, Brigadiers, and the Sieur Verboom Engineer General. Orders are given for the fpeedy repairing the Caftle of *Ter Veur*, where an Apartment is to be got ready for the Duke of Burgundy, who is coming into this Countrey to Command as Generaliffimo this Campaign. On Friday laft the Marquifs of Bedmar went to Ghent, where he is to receive on Sunday next, the Homage from the States of Flanders in the Name of His Catholick Majefty.

From the Amfterdam Gazette, Dated March 16.

Vienna, March 1. The Emperour has refolved to difpofe of the Confifcated Eftates of the Hungarian Rebels, and apply the Produce of them to the Charge of the War; They are valued at three Millions of Crowns.

Francfort, March 8. The French Envoy in his Speech to the Deputies of the Circle of Franconia, in the Diet held at Nuremberg, having rudely tax'd the Emperour with infringing the Peace, they broke up without admitting him again into their Affembly.

Harwich, March 10. At Six a Clock in the Evening Yefterday, fail'd the Eagle Pacquet-Boat with a Meffenger and an Exprefs for Holland: And this Morning a hired Smack fail'd with a Second Exprefs for Holland.

London, March 12. The Right Honourable the Earl of Marlborough is declared Captain General of the Forces in England and Holland.

When the King's Body was laid out, there was found a Bracelet about his Right Arm, with His Queen's Wedding Ring on it. He was open'd on Tuefday Morning, his Brain was in very good order, but there was hardly any Blood left in the Body, and his Lungs were very bad.

ADVERTISEMENT.

it crossed the Atlantic. While articles in these papers were concerned strictly with informing the public, the papers were soon joined by another, *The New-England Courant*, founded by James Franklin (brother of Benjamin Franklin), which sought to entertain as much as to inform.

The 19th century saw the rise of the "penny press," or American newspapers that cost only a penny—a price affordable to nearly everyone. As newspaper readership increased, newspapers became involved in an intense competition for wider circulation. By the end of the 1800s, such competition had sparked "yellow journalism," a brand of reporting characterized by sensational stories of gossip, crime, and scandal designed to grab readers' attention. These stories were printed under huge headlines known as "scare heads," which often suggested exaggerated importance for relatively minor events.

The following article was printed on the front page of Joseph Pulitzer's "yellow" New York paper, *The Evening World*, under the large headline "STRANGE DOUBLE LIFE OF MAN REVEALED BY TRAGEDY" (January 6, 1900). As you read, think about whether you would classify this story as an example of yellow journalism.

A remarkable sequel to the Mount Vernon tragedy of a week ago came to light to-day.

"Prof. Alfred Morrison," the teacher of languages in Mount Vernon who, while dreaming of burglars a week ago last Thursday night shot and killed his young wife, was not Prof. Alfred Morrison.

That was an assumed name. He was leading a double life.

His real name is Frederick Gordon. He has a wife whom he married eighteen years ago....

She told the story of his duplicity this morning to an Evening World reporter, and her husband, who still lives in Mount Vernon and is half-crazed by the tragedy of last week, corroborated every word of it.

It is a remarkable story—the more surprising that a man could deceive two women for so many years, neither suspecting his duplicity and his sin not being found out until in his dream he killed one of the two women he successfully deceived so long.

The wronged wife was interviewed by an Evening World reporter in two poor little rooms at 1456 Third Avenue....

"I never dreamed that my husband was leading a double life until some one told me about two weeks ago that he was going with another woman in Mount Vernon. I told Fred this and he denied it."

"Last Saturday I read in The Evening World the story of the Morrison shooting. I recognized the picture of Morrison as that of my husband."...

Gordon was like a maniac when he heard that his double life had been disclosed at last. He tore his hair and stamped about the room in awful rage as he told the full story, declaring that he was crazy, that his father and mother had died of suffering of the brain and that the same fate awaited him.

Although this type of sensational story was
typical of yellow newspapers, many of these papers
(including Pulitzer's) also covered serious, con-
sequential news. At the same time, they shaped the
newspapers of the future, including today's, with
their emphasis on crime and scandal and their use
of banner headlines and large pictures. During the
early years of the 20th century, many newspapers
began to publish crusades for reform. Although
most of these crusades—which included disaster
relief campaigns and efforts to expose political
corruption—were another attempt at increasing
circulation, they did in fact help to bring about
reform, such as the creation of `antitrust` laws.
Crusading journalists were known as muckrakers.

By the time World War I broke out in 1914, muck-
raking and yellow journalism had lost their popular-
ity. Hundreds of newspaper and magazine journalists
were sent to Europe to cover the war, as they were
again 25 years later during World War II. After
these wars, many journalists felt an increasing
need to provide more than `objective` facts, and
interpretation became a regular part of feature
stories and editorial columns. Reporters also tried

to make their writing clear and simple, explaining difficult concepts so that readers could understand the news. During the 1960s and '70s, a group of journalists (later known as "New Journalists") began to use `fictional` devices such as description, scenes, and dialogue in reporting their painstakingly researched news stories. New Journalists had a lasting impact on nonfiction writing, and the techniques they developed are still used by a number of journalists, especially in magazines.

Today, the circulation of many newspapers and magazines is declining as people increasingly turn to television and the Internet for more of their information needs. Online newspapers are gaining in prominence, however, giving readers access to continuously updated news accounts from a variety of news sources around the world. All you have to do is pick up a newspaper (or click on one) to find out what's happening around you today!

The word "news," of course, implies something
that is new. In fact, the word "journalism" comes
from the French term *jour*, which means "day" or
"daily." Yet "new" or "daily" can mean something
that has happened relatively recently or that
happened in the past but has new relevance today.

Although there is no universal definition of
what constitutes news, journalists generally
look for "news values" in determining whether a
story warrants a spot in a newspaper or magazine.
Stories that will likely be considered news have
a wide impact, are relevant to readers, happened
nearby, feature prominent individuals, occurred
recently, involve conflict, or feature something
unusual. Not all stories will have all of these
values, but most stories will have at least one—
otherwise readers may not bother with them. After
all, there's not much excitement in (or need to
read) a story about traffic flowing smoothly and
without incident in a city far from where you
live. But a story about a car accident that causes
a two-hour traffic delay down the block from your
house is likely to hold your interest.

Most stories about something that has just

happened are presented as "hard news." Hard news provides facts about an event, giving readers the essentials in an objective story. It usually does not attempt to set an event in `context` or analyze what its consequences might be.

Providing context or analysis are tasks left to feature articles. Although features are often called "soft news," they can cover topics as serious as those covered by hard news. In fact, feature stories are often an expansion of hard news stories, offering insight into an event's background or explaining and analyzing complicated stories more fully. Unlike hard news stories, which generally focus on just the facts, features can delve into the emotional side of stories (although they do need to include facts as well).

The feature category encompasses a wide variety of article types. Among the most popular today, especially in magazines, are the celebrity profile and the how-to article—which can tell readers how to do everything from saving money to making small talk. Many newspapers and magazines also include "human interest" stories about ordinary people in extraordinary circumstances. A feature article might present one woman's battle with cancer, for example, or the story of one family's escape from their burning home. Travel stories, book or movie reviews, and columns dispensing opinions or advice can also be considered features.

Some feature stories are investigative in nature. They present the work of a journalist who has thoroughly scrutinized an institution or person and uncovered previously unknown information important to the reading public. Investigative pieces often reveal corruption or danger, as in the following excerpt from an article by muckraker William Hard. Hard investigated working conditions at the United States Steel Corporation in Chicago, revealing his findings in the article "Making Steel and Killing Men," published in *Everybody's Magazine* in 1907. Hard begins his article with a description of the factory and the fact that 46 workers were killed there in 1906. He goes on to write:

A worker in an early 20th-century steel factory

When the American Institute of Social Service tells us that 536,165 Americans are killed or maimed every year in American industry, our minds are merely stunned. But the specific case of Ora Allen, on the twelfth day of December 1906 has a poignant thrust that goes through the stunned mind to the previously untouched recesses of the heart....

On the twelfth of last December Newton Allen was operating overhead crane No. 3.... Seated aloft in the cage of his crane, he dropped his chains and hooks to the men beneath and carried pots and ladles up and down the length of the pouring-floor. That floor ... was edged, all along one side, by a row of open-hearth furnaces, fourteen of them, and in each one there were sixty-four tons of white, boiling iron, boiling into steel. From these furnaces the white-hot metal, now steel, was withdrawn and poured into big ten-ton molds....

Newton Allen, up in the cage of his 100-ton electric crane, was requested by a ladleman from below to pick up a pot and carry it to another part of the floor. This pot was filled with the hot slag that is the refuse left over when the pure steel has been run off.

Newton Allen let down the hooks of his crane. The ladleman attached those hooks to the pot. Newton Allen started down the floor. Just as he started, one of the hooks slipped.... [He] hurried back to the scene of the accident. He saw a man lying on his face. He heard him screaming. He saw that he was being roasted by the slag that had poured out of the pot. He ran up to him and turned him over.

"At that time," said Newton Allen, ... "I did not know it was my brother."

As you read, what struck you most about this article? Was it the fact that 536,165 Americans were killed or injured on the job every year during the first part of the 20th century? Or was it the story of Ora and Newton Allen? That story is packed with emotion, and it touches us as stark statistics—no matter how shocking—never could. Hard goes on to present details of the other scenes of death at the steel company, and in doing so he not only presents a gripping tale but alerts readers to a shocking reality. As a result of Hard's investigative feature, as well as articles about occupational safety by other muckrakers, factories began to adopt new safety rules, and state workers' compensation laws were passed.

Although investigative stories are usually hard-hitting, feature stories do not have to be about serious topics. In fact, many feature stories are written more to entertain readers than to inform them of life-changing news. So look at the world around you and think about what you'd like to know more about—chances are feature readers would, too!

Although you may think of journalists as writers (which they certainly are), much of a journalist's job happens before he or she ever sits down to write a word. Journalists must carefully research every article they write in order to gather the information needed to answer the six news questions: who, what, where, when, why, and how. Depending on how much time they have, journalists can use documents and public records, interviews, and personal observation as sources for their articles. If you were going to write a story about your school district's decision to cut the art program, for example, what types of research might you conduct? You could check government records to find out how many other school districts have cut art programs. You might interview the art teacher and several art students, as well as a member of the school board. If your story were a feature article, in which you would have space to explore the subject more fully, you might even spend some time observing an art class.

Once your research is complete, the writing can finally begin. How you write a news story depends very much on what type of story it is.

Although feature articles offer a great deal of flexibility in their structure, most have a clear beginning, middle, and end. The introduction to a news story is called a lead. Feature leads can include a quote, a description, a story, or anything else that will grab the reader's attention and convince him or her to continue. Following the lead, many feature stories have a billboard paragraph (referred to by many names, including summary graph, nut graph, or signal graph). The billboard acts as a road sign, summarizing the point of your article and letting readers know what to expect as they read on. The body of a feature article can be organized in chronological order, as a narrative, around a theme, or in any other format that allows you to present your subject clearly. The conclusion of a feature (sometimes called the kicker) wraps up the story in a powerful way. The kicker can use a quote, a summary, a story, or a warning—whatever will leave your reader with a lasting impression.

Unlike feature articles, hard news stories generally follow a standard format known as the inverted pyramid, and there is little room for

U.S. newspapers announcing political news in 1956

variation within this form. Stories written as an inverted pyramid present the most important information first, followed by paragraphs of lesser and lesser importance. Readers can get the essence of a hard news story simply by reading the lead (although a few hard news stories use an attention-grabbing lead before jumping into the most important facts of the story). Hard news stories do not have a conclusion; they simply stop when all of the information has been related.

The following hard news story was printed in *The New York Times* on February 26, 1922, under the headline "RACING STOLEN AUTO SMASHES CITY BUS; ONE DEAD, 20 HURT." As you read it, think about how it might have been written differently if it were a feature story.

𝔗𝔥𝔢 𝔑𝔢𝔴 𝔜𝔬𝔯𝔨 𝔗𝔦𝔪𝔢𝔰

A policeman was killed and twenty or thirty persons, many of them children, suffered broken bones, cuts and bruises late last night when a touring car, probably stolen, smashed into a crowded municipal automobile bus at Madison and Roosevelt Streets.

Despite the crash, which wrecked both vehicles and threw the passengers of the heavy bus into a maimed, tangled heap, the occupants of the touring car escaped. A general police alarm was sent out for them and patrolmen all over the city were on the alert early this morning. At the same time a close watch was kept on hospitals in the belief that the man, or men, in the touring car could not have gone unscathed.

The policeman who was killed when the bus toppled on him as he was about to alight to report for duty, was Thomas O'Keefe of the Grand Avenue Station, Brooklyn....

Nathan Blitz was driving the bus west on Madison Street toward the Chambers Street ferry. There were about forty persons in it, at least half of them children, returning with their parents from the movies and other Saturday night diversions....

Blitz was slowing the bus for the customary stop on the far side of the street when he saw a big Marmon car bearing down upon him, full speed. [The article then gives details of the crash and rescue efforts before continuing.]...

The detectives believe the fatal haste of the automobile driver was due to fear that he was being pursued, and they were examining all stolen car reports early this morning....

Patrolman O'Keefe was 30 years old. He lived at 190 Monroe Street, Manhattan, with a wife and several children. His relatives were notified in preparation for sending the body home.

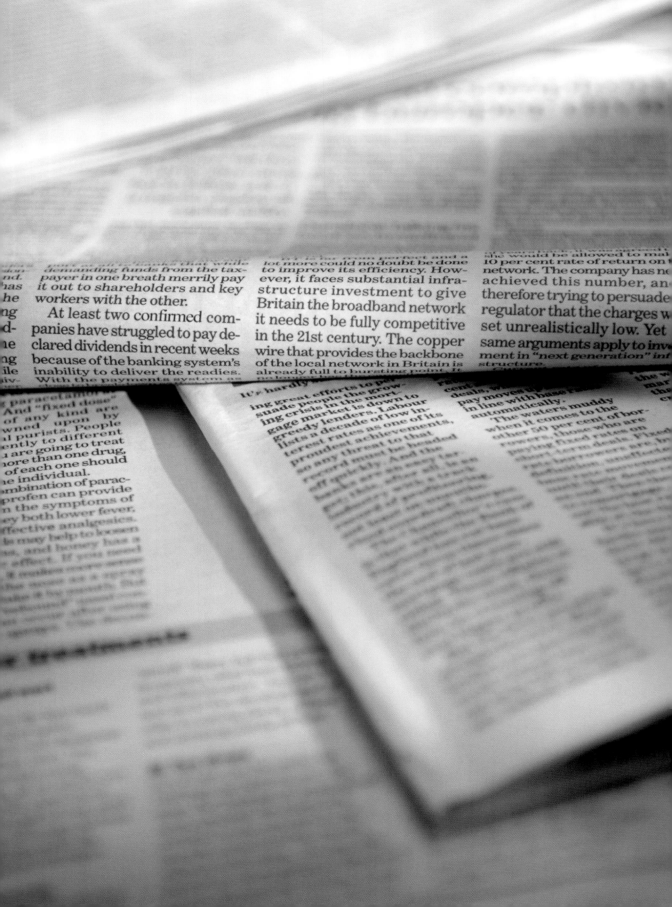

demanding funds from the tax-
payer in one breath merrily pay
it out to shareholders and key
workers with the other.

At least two confirmed com-
panies have struggled to pay declared dividends in recent weeks
because of the banking system's
inability to deliver the readies.
With the payments system as

lot more could no doubt be done
to improve its efficiency. However, it faces substantial infra-
structure investment to give
Britain the broadband network
it needs to be fully competitive
in the 21st century. The copper
wire that provides the backbone
of the local network in Britain is
already full to bursting point. It

she would be allowed to ma
10 per cent rate of return on t
network. The company has ne
achieved this number, an
therefore trying to persuade
regulator that the charges w
set unrealistically low. Yet
same arguments apply to inv
ment in "next generation" inf
structure.

paracetamol
And "fixed dose
of any kind are
wned upon by
ll purists. People
ently to different
l are going to treat
ore than one drug,
of each one should
he individual.
mbination of parac-
profen can provide
n the symptoms of
ey both lower fever.
ffective analgesics.
s may help to loosen
s, and honey has a
effect. If you need

It's hardly to
ing great efforts to per-
suade people the grow-
ing crisis in the mort-
gage market is down to
greedy lenders. Labour
lists a decade of low in-
terest rates as one of its
proudest achievements,
so any threat to that
record must be headed
off quickly. And the

deals, w
cent
pay moves
in line with base
automatically.
The waters muddy
when it comes to the
other 50 per cent of bor-
rowers, those who are
paying fixed rates on
short-term deals. Fixed-
rate borrowers are be

Look back at the lead of this story. What did the
journalist who wrote it (like many hard news stories, this one has no `byline`) consider to be the
most important facts? Notice that the lead answers
four news questions immediately: who (a police
officer and 20 or 30 others), what (were injured in
a car-bus accident), where (Madison and Roosevelt
Streets), and when (late last night). How the accident actually occurred isn't covered until the
middle of the story, and why is left for the end.
The last two paragraphs present the least important
information. If they were cut from the story (or if
a busy reader decided not to read all the way to the
end), it would have little impact on the article's
overall meaning.

Although this article is more than 80 years old,
it reads much like the hard news stories in today's
newspapers. That's because the inverted pyramid
form has changed little in the 150 years since it
was developed. So find out what's happening right
now, figure out what's most important about it, and
construct your own upside-down pyramid of words!

Much of what ends up in the news is basically the same as what has been there before. Accidents happen every day. Sports teams win or lose nearly every night. City councils hold meetings once a month. That does not mean that journalists can simply pull out an old article about a similar event, change some names, and present it as a new story, though. Each article needs to present the specifics about the event it is covering, and, ideally, it should make clear how this event is different from other events of its kind.

For hard news, especially, the most basic elements of a story are the facts. Where, precisely, did the accident occur? What, exactly, was the score of the baseball game? What, specifically, did the city council decide? But a story that presented fact after fact after fact would likely soon bore readers. That's why many articles—both hard news and features—also include quotes. Quotes not only break up long blocks of reporting but also provide `credibility`, helping to confirm the information you have included. This does not mean that a quote should say the same thing as what you've already written, though. Quotes need to add something new

to the story. And quotes should be interesting—
either because of what a person said or how he or
she said it.

Quotes are not the only way to add interest to
an article. Anecdotes can help to illustrate a
point by telling a story. For example, if your article is about children skipping school, you might
include an anecdote or two about kids who have found
a way to get out of school for the day. The anecdotes can give your story a more human touch than
pure statistics on truancy rates could.

Quotation marks, which clue
readers to spoken lines

Descriptions can also help bring readers into a story. You don't necessarily need to describe a whole scene (although you might choose to in a feature story). A few telling details can help readers see your story clearly. Telling details help you to follow the writing advice, "Show, don't tell." For example, rather than writing that a tornado was destructive, you might write that a child's teddy bear lies in a field, a crib is tangled in a tree, or a car rests on the roof of a house. Those telling details will help readers see the specific destruction caused by this specific tornado.

The following excerpt comes from journalist Sydney H. Schanberg's Pulitzer Prize-winning article "In a Besieged Cambodian City, Hunger, Death and the Whimpering of Children" (January 16, 1975). As you read, try to pick out the quotes, anecdotes, and telling details that make this story compelling.

Hungry children in the war-torn nation of Cambodia in 1975

Every fifteen minutes or so a shell screams down and explodes in this besieged town and another half-dozen people are killed or wounded. It goes on day and night.

The tile floors of the military infirmary and civilian hospital are slippery with blood. They have long since run out of painkilling drugs. Bodies are everywhere—some people half conscious crying out in pain, some with gaping wounds who will not live. Some are already dead....

Inside the infirmary a seven-year-old girl, a filthy bandage over the wound in her stomach, lies on a wooden table. The only doctor in the town feels her pulse. It is failing.

Suddenly her father appears, a soldier. He has come from the spot where another of his children, a five-year-old girl, has just been killed by a mortar shell....

"I love all my children," is all he says as he walks away with the dying child—heading for the helicopters that are too few to carry all the wounded to Phnom Penh....

The thirty thousand or more refugees who have fled to Neak Luong from outlying areas as the Communist-led insurgents have advanced toward the town have been reduced to subsistence on the thinnest of rice gruel....

"They're going to have to airdrop more food," said one disheartened relief worker. "That's all there is to it. Otherwise people will starve."...

Amid all this, there was at times a preposterous normality.

In the market, where a few Chinese-run shops were open for those who still had money, a colonel who had just flown in with his fresh troops was examining a bottle of French cologne with a discriminating air. His boots were highly polished, his uniform starched, his neck scarf just so. He squeezed the atomizer, sniffed the spray, then put it back and walked away disdainfully.

As you read this, did you almost feel as if you were in the Asian country of Cambodia, witnessing the horrors of war? Yet at no point does Schanberg tell us that this is a horrible scene. Instead, he shows us, beginning with the opening anecdote that relates the heart-wrenching story of the father

A Cambodian soldier
carrying a wounded boy

33

who is about to lose his second child. Although Schanberg uses few quotes, the ones he has chosen are powerful. The father's quote allows us to hear his pain, and the quote from the relief worker provides evidence to back up the assertion that people are barely surviving on the food they have.

Schanberg has made us feel as if we are in this specific Cambodian village without ever once describing the entire scene. He doesn't tell us about the village's buildings. Nowhere does he mention its streets or vegetation or waterways. Instead, telling details show us the destruction of the village. The floors are "slippery with blood," the girl wears a "filthy bandage," and a shell "screams down" (notice that telling details can use any of the senses). And the telling details about the colonel sniffing French cologne—boots "highly polished," uniform "starched," and neck scarf "just so"—show us what Schanberg means when he writes that there was also a "preposterous normality." So use your powers of observation to pick out the anecdotes, quotes, and telling details of life, and then write them into a news story that readers won't be able to put down.

Most people's view of the world is shaped at least in part by what they read on the pages of newspapers and magazines. They put their trust in journalists, who, in turn, have an obligation to make their stories as accurate and reliable as possible. One of the easiest ways to prevent inaccuracies from creeping into a story is to double-check all facts. Any information that is uncertain should be presented as such. Many crime stories, for example, state that a suspect "allegedly" mugged a pedestrian. This clues readers in to the fact that this suspect may or may not have committed the crime; he or she may be charged or convicted at a later date.

Checking facts and noting uncertainty are only part of providing accurate information, however. Writers should also strive to provide fair, balanced, `unbiased` coverage. Although it is impossible for anyone to be completely objective (after all, we all have opinions), hard news journalists try to avoid letting their opinions show. Although features generally offer more opportunity for writers to take a stance, opinions should be presented as just that, and not passed off for fact. In general, news stories also try to present both sides of controversial issues.

Just because every journalist is obligated to write the truth doesn't mean that every journalist writes in the same way. If you and a friend were both assigned to write a feature on a recent movie, for example, you would likely produce two very different articles, not only because of *what* you wrote, but because of *how* you wrote it. In general, feature articles allow for more individual `style` than do hard news stories. As you read a feature, you can tell that it was written by a specific journalist—an individual. Hard news stories, on the other hand, are usually written in the style of the specific newspaper in which they appear, known as the institutional style. At most newspapers, a clear, simple style with short words, short sentences, and short paragraphs dominates hard news articles.

Both hard news and feature stories are generally written in the `third person` point of view, although feature stories about events that have happened to you personally can be written in the `first person` (using "I"). Even when you write in the third person, though, your feelings can come through in your `tone`. Hard news stories generally adopt a neutral tone, but feature articles can have a compassionate, humorous, outraged, or ironic tone (or any other tone that expresses the writer's attitude toward his or her subject). Tone should match the subject matter, though. Terminal diseases shouldn't be treated as a joke, for example. Pay attention to the tone of the following excerpt from the article "How to Lie with Statistics" (August 1950) by American writer Darrell Huff. Is the style of this excerpt distinct from the others in this book?

"The average Yaleman, Class of '24," Time *magazine reported last year after reading something in the New York Sun, a newspaper published in those days, "makes $25,111 a year."*

Well, good for him!

But, come to think of it, what does this improbably precise ... figure mean? Is it, as it appears to be, evidence that if you send your boy to Yale you won't have to work in your old age and neither will he? Is this average a mean or is it a median? What kind of sample is it based on? You could lump one Texas oilman with two hundred hungry freelance writers and report their *average income as $25,000-odd a year. The arithmetic is impeccable, the figure is convincingly precise, and the amount of meaning there is in it you could put in your eye.*

In just such ways is the secret language of statistics, so appealing in a fact-minded culture, being used to sensationalize, inflate, confuse, and oversimplify....

Here are some of the ways it is done.

The sample with the built-in bias. *Our Yale men—or Yalemen, as they say in the Time-Life building—belong to this flourishing group.... At least two interesting categories of 1924-model Yale men have been excluded.*

First there are those whose present addresses are unknown to their classmates. Wouldn't you bet that these lost sheep are earning less than the boys from prominent families and the others who can be handily reached from a Wall Street office?

There are those who chucked the questionnaire into the nearest wastebasket. Maybe they didn't answer because they were not making enough money to brag about. Like the fellow who found a note clipped to his first pay check suggesting that he consider the amount of his salary confidential: "Don't worry," he told the boss. "I'm just as ashamed of it as you are."

Huff's style in this piece is relaxed and informal, with `colloquial` phrases such as "wouldn't you bet" and "chucked the questionnaire." Although he is dealing with statistics, a potentially dry subject, Huff adopts a lighthearted, humorous tone. That tone is not out of line with the topic, however, since Huff is not trying to teach us the

An early-1900s illustration
of Yale University students

complicated math behind statistics but is instead trying to expose the ways that statistics are sometimes misused to prove a point. In fact, Huff's tone helps to make his article not only readable but also enjoyable. He even goes so far as to add a joke to his piece. Despite the chuckles this article may elicit, though, it also helps readers understand a serious point: you can't believe every number you read.

Whether humorous or serious, formal or informal, hard or soft, news stories have the power to show readers the world in which they live. Without such stories, it would be difficult to find out what was happening around the world, across the country, or maybe even on the other side of town. The best news stories have the power to touch not only our brains but also our hearts. So open your eyes to the news that is happening around you—and then open readers' eyes to it, too!

A typewriter, a machine used by journalists for more than a century

Telling the Type

Newspapers generally provide a combination of hard news stories and features, while magazines print primarily feature stories. Learn to distinguish between the two by picking up a copy of a local or national daily newspaper (most weeklies tend to focus on features). Read through the stories on the front page. Are they mostly hard news or features? Now open to the inside. Is the proportion of features and hard news the same here? Are the feature articles based on the day's hard news stories, or are they unrelated? After you've read through several pages of the newspaper, pick out your favorite story. What is it that draws you to this story: the information it relates, a compelling narrative, or the journalist's style? If your choice is a hard news story, try to rewrite it as a feature; if it's a feature, turn it into hard news.

Learning about the World

Journalists generally rely on three types of sources—documents, interviews, and observations—to gather the necessary information to write their stories. In order to familiarize yourself with using documents, try to find statistics on the population of your city or town (and don't rely on population signs posted at the city limits, which can be out of date). Then, practice interviewing. Choose a prominent local figure (a teacher, city official, or police officer, for example) and ask if you can interview him or her. Before you go to the interview, make a list of questions to ask, and take notes during the interview. Be sure to write down any quotes you might like to use word-for-word. Finally, hone your powers of observation by sitting in a crowded public space and paying attention to what is going on around you. Make note of telling details—what makes this public space and the people in it different from anywhere else?

Stylish News

Writing news articles is different from writing essays, short stories, or any other writing assignment, and it can take practice. In order to get used to writing in a news style, take a familiar story and turn it into an article. First, think about your favorite children's book; better yet, reread it to make sure that you have all the details straight. Now, write a hard news or feature article about the story. Remember to follow the inverted pyramid if you're writing a hard news story. If you choose to write a feature, make sure you have a compelling lead, a well-organized body, and a powerful kicker. You do not need to include every fact from the story; choose only those that you think are newsworthy. When you have finished, reread your article. Does it present a fair and accurate account of the story? Is it compelling?

Truth Detector

Although journalists try to maintain objectivity
in their hard news stories, sometimes biases and
opinions show through their writing. Choose a
local daily newspaper and read at least 10 hard
news stories published in it. Do you think the
stories present fair and balanced coverage of
their subject? If not, circle any questionable
sections. Pay attention to unclear language,
statements of opinion, and uneven coverage of
controversial issues. Also look at the individual
words of the stories. Sometimes, seemingly innocent
`adjectives` may reflect a judgment on the part
of the journalist. (Calling someone "brilliant,"
for example, reflects not fact but opinion.) After
you've finished analyzing the hard news stories,
read several articles in a magazine. Do these
articles seem to reflect more opinions than the
hard news stories? When opinions are stated, is it
apparent that they are opinions and not statements
of fact?

LOSSARY

adjectives words that describe people, places, or things

anecdotes brief stories recounting specific incidents or events

antitrust opposed to monopolies (in which one company obtains complete control over a specific product or service and operates without competition) in order to prevent unfair business practices

byline a line at the beginning of an article that provides the writer's name

chronological following the order of time; something that is related chronologically tells what happened first, then what happened next, and so on

colloquial characteristic of informal spoken language or conversation

context the circumstances that surround something (or someone) and within which it exists

credibility the quality of inspiring belief; a credible journalist is one readers trust as reliable

fictional having to do with literary works in which situations, characters, and events are made up; novels and short stories are works of fiction

first person a perspective, pronoun, or verb form that refers to the speaker or writer; in English, "I" and "we" are first-person pronouns

narrative a story, as opposed to exposition (which generally provides background information)

nonfiction writing that is based on facts rather than fiction

objective based on facts and uninfluenced by opinion or personal feelings

style the way in which an author writes, as distinct from what he or she writes

third person a perspective, pronoun, or verb form that refers to someone or something being spoken about; in English, third person pronouns include "he," "she," "it," and "they"

tone the attitude of an author toward his or her subject

unbiased fair and without prejudice (preformed, unfavorable opinions of someone or something founded on incomplete information or unreasonable feelings)

SELECTED BIBLIOGRAPHY

Cappon, Rene J. *The Associated Press Guide to News Writing*. Foster City, Calif.: IDG Books Worldwide, 2000.

Hamilton, Nancy M. *Magazine Writing: A Step-by-Step Guide for Success*. Boston: Pearson Education, 2007.

Mott, Frank Luther. *American Journalism: A History: 1690–1960*. New York: Macmillan Company, 1962.

Ricketson, Matthew. *Writing Feature Stories: How to Research and Write Newspaper and Magazine Articles*. Crows Nest, New South Wales, Australia: Allen & Unwin, 2004.

Wilson, John M. *The Complete Guide to Magazine Article Writing*. Cincinnati, Ohio: Writer's Digest Books, 1993.

Zinsser, William. *On Writing Well: The Classic Guide to Writing Nonfiction*. New York: HarperCollins, 1994.

⒤NDEX